HUNTED CARRION

Sonnets to a Stalker

Also by Anne Champion

Reluctant Mistress (Gold Wake Press)
The Dark Length Home (Noctuary Press)
The Good Girl is Always a Ghost (Black Lawrence Press)
Book of Levitations (Trembling Pillow Press)
She Saints & Holy Profanities (Quarterly West)

HUNTED CARRION

Sonnets to a Stalker

Anne Champion

ACKNOWLEDGEMENTS

Burningword Literary Journal: "The Empath"
Chiron Review: "Self Blame," "Watching *Ancient Aliens* with my
      Rapist," and "Processing Trauma While Thinking About
      My Childhood Boyfriend Who Killed Himself"
Connecticut River Review: "Happy Birthday, Dear Rapist"
Hawaii Pacific Review: "Hunted Carrion"
Live Nude Poems: "Stigmata" and "Corpse Bride"
Medium: "Survivor" and "A Borderline's Lucid Dreaming"
Ninth Letter: "Triggered Memories: Grief"
Pembroke Magazine: "Death"
The Pinch: "Is it a Dream or"
Poetry South: "Echo and Narcissus"
River Styx: "Isolating"
Rogue Agent: "The Hunter"
Thrush Poetry Journal: "Time"
Verse Daily: "Isolating"

"Happy Birthday, Dear Rapist" and "Time" were nominated for a
Pushcart Prize.

CONTENTS

To L—

We're friends, right?

PROLOGUE

For eight months, between 2021-2022, I was stalked by the maintenance director of my apartment. He broke my appliances to spend time with me, and we developed a friendship, but I began avoiding him because he spoke poorly about his wife and I thought he wanted to cheat. I was 40, six years celibate, and wise enough to know nothing good comes from that kind of situation.

I didn't anticipate that he had installed a microphone in my apartment, so he heard me discussing my thoughts with my therapist and friends, and he didn't handle the rejection well.

Shortly after, I was drugged and sexually assaulted for several weeks.

He broke in through my screen door at night with a crow bar after drugging my Brita water filter in my refrigerator when I was at work.

During the trauma, I was disoriented in a drugged fog. The cognitive dissonance and shock were profound. I was vomiting, losing simple short term memory, suffering severe headaches, sweating through my sheets, unconscious for half the days, unsure of reality, engaging in confusing and contradictory interactions with him, and waking with genital pain and flashes of memories almost too painful to process.

After I fled and reported, I was homeless in hotels in withdrawals while I came to terms with how I'd been stalked. I'd found evidence of the microphone and crow bar marks on my screen door along with places he wrote in my journals. I soon realized he'd shared all the settings on my phone to his and was tracking me.

I was gang stalked and threatened several times for a few months following police and lawyer contact: he found my new location.

My stalker is still free, a deeply troubled man, a shadow that trails my life forever. But he's no stranger to prison: he first went as a teenager.

The system didn't protect me or reform him.

1 in 3 women and 1 in 6 men will be stalked in their lifetime. 81% of women who were stalked were also physically assaulted (CDC).

***

He wasn't my first rape, but he was the most severe and traumatic.

To survive, I needed to understand: I went into a deep dive study of the mental health of rapists and sociopathy.

He collapsed me and made me look hard at the rubble of my past—at a pattern of violent men, one that went back to my father, and beyond—a masculine wound I've sat too close to, one that pulls at me relentlessly, threatening to swallow me in its black hole…

…a generational, spiritual wound, from the roots through the branches of family trees, a pattern of abuses and violences in the families of the boys of my youth whose pain took me out— through their assaults, their suicides, their prison sentences, their hellfire of barely-contained rage.

These wounded boys, these sins of the fathers: what generational curse followed my life?

This man walked into my apartment to fix my fuse, and I thought he was a garden snake.

Before I knew it, I had a python wrapped around my neck.

The rapists, the racists, the misogynists, the homophobes, the transphobes, the fascists, the broken, broken boys…

…the secrets, the shames, the manipulations, the hate, the perversions, the abusers with the most convincing masks.

According to a National Epidemiologic Survey on Alcohol and Related Conditions of psychiatric disorders of 43,000 Americans, 8.4% of the population has sociopathic traits, such as a lack of empathy and conscience, making it the second most common mental illness for Americans next to depression (*Bad Boys, Bad Men: Confronting Antisocial Personality Disorder*, Donald W. Black).

Antisocial Personality Disorder and Narcissistic Personality Disorder are the least funded mental health disorders for research in America.

I've lived in the blinking gaslights of a denied public mental health crisis. My stalker woke me up, a dark miracle that infected my whole spirit. My life burned to cinders, and I had to transform my ashes into something that could fly out of fire.

5

This book is the raw and vulnerable grappling of an all too common extreme trauma. Writing it kept me alive. I hope it can help others who feel muzzled or broken by this type of pain and betrayal.

The only justice I seek is to speak my truth.

And to say it in poetry, my native tongue for despair, and in sonnets, a form traditionally used to express love.

Despite everything, I still believe love is the antidote.

KNOCK KNOCK: MEET YOUR RAPIST

When I opened the door to your face, it was as startling
as a flash of lightning striking too near. The temporary blindness,
the withering to humility that only divine power can evoke.
One needs no language to read the shaky glowing scrawl
across the sky that only a demented, selfish god can boom.
Your voice said, *I heard you needed a new fuse.* But your smile
said tempest, said thunderclap, said the pleading of siren wails,
said the shrieks of an inner child, huddled
in a corner, bruised and shivering, wondering
if a wolf will lead her to shelter or to a pack.
When the bolt strikes her spine, she splits in half,
momentarily voiceless, before she realizes her branches
are aflame, before she learns that lightning can unearth
and scorch even the deepest, rot-infested roots.

THE HUNTER

The day you installed the microphone, you'd broken my heater,
feigned ignorance of how to fix it. For hours, you unraveled pieces

of yourself as cautiously as the wires you twisted. I handed empathy
like I was passing tools—the more I gave, the more you confessed:

your childhood home's dirt floor; your alcoholic father; the drive-by;
the teenage prison sentence; the men who tattooed your testicles.

I must've done something bad in a past life to deserve this life. I didn't fear you.
Have you ever seen that show about a stalker? you asked. *Dark,* I replied.

The more you unfurled, the closer you moved towards me.
When your arm touched mine as you pressed against me

to show pictures on your phone, it felt like an electric zap.
There you were, palms gripping horned beasts slayed.

I had no idea I'd soon be the carcass you gripped, the empty-eyed,
slack-bodied picture on your phone, the proof of power in your palm.

IS IT A DREAM OR

When raped while drugged, the body loses all borders;
the protective fortresses of the mind are abandoned, the life
collapses on itself like a great empire, the relics
get buried beneath miles of stone. You'll excavate the ruins

of your earliest histories of pain for years
after the invader takes his victory, shaft to center.

Where did my brain go when you impaled me?
I see the enemy only in flashes: a soldier in my kitchen,

a monster in my bed. When raped while drugged, memories blur
to dream: the long trusted ally of the body revolts,
a Judas kiss. My mind keeps replaying myself waking in orgasm,
your face hovering, a look of stun-gun shock—surprise

and fear—as if you were the prey. Then, another vision: you're crying
as you rape, calling me *mama*—as if it's *your* inner child under attack.

ANALYZING YOU ONCE AGAIN

After you first raped me, you asked if I thought I was capable
of violence. I know now what you wanted to know: if I was conscious,
would I fight? Would I kill you for what you did when the GHB fog
lifted? I replied that I could feel violence boiling in my belly like a pit
of tar. You looked like a child the way you stared at me then.
I asked the question back. You chuckled, said the man before me
is not who you always are. I was unaware I was bayoneted

already, though my cunt was ripped, my head fogged.
You said a man once almost shot you while hunting.
You became something animal—you leapt through
the brush and tackled him with your gun to his temple.
He's lucky to be alive, you said. So was I. But where did I misaim

and spook you to attack? Or is it that my love is like the moon,
shapeshifting men of a certain curse into starving wolves?

WAYS TO CONSOLE

At least
he didn't kill
my cats.

At least
he didn't give me
a disease.

At least
I'm still
alive.

Scratch that.

It would've been
easier
not to have
survived.

PTSD

Yesterday, my students made me laugh.
I thought about how long it'd been since
I laughed, how children wrench it from me best,
how love always blooms in me like a stubborn fungus.

I thought about how no matter who I love now,
half my heart will always be infested with your rot.

A car pulled up, and it was you—
that green jacket, hunter's camouflage.
I thought coolly:
one of us will die now.

A child stepped out of the car—
a child. Not you.

Is that how I always saw you? Is that how
you contaminated me, disarmed me with laughter?

TIME

A student mentioned that if we could space travel 100,000 light years
and look back at earth, we'd see dinosaurs: that's how long it'd take
for the light to reach back. Just as some stars are merely memories of
the universe whose light is only now pinpricking us. Just then,

all time collapsed, as I realized that from a certain distance in space,
you're always raping me, always taking a crow bar to my door, always
standing over my bed, and I'm always incapacitated, vulnerable.

I wonder if time can collapse in the opposite direction too—
if from some distance in space, we're already dead.

Is this why I felt that surge of recognition, as if I'd known you always,
as if something inside you was dead, as if I could re-animate you
by feeding myself to the zombie? Is this why I still think of you daily,

why emotions wax and wane as consistent as the moon, as if you were
the darkness that comes to swallow the star's last gasp of light?

WATCHING *YOU* AFTER BEING STALKED

I saw from the beginning that the stalking victim was going to get killed
by the man who professed to love her madly, to want to protect her.

Maybe before you happened, there was a recognition of myself
I couldn't admit, avoided, because when I finally watched, I vomited.

(Remember how much I puked from the drugs you gave me?
I hope the smell stays with you too). I didn't realize the main character

was a poet (like me), that she was surrounded by toxic people
she mistakenly loved (like me), that she had a messed up childhood

(like me, like you), that she really wanted to be seen and loved (like me,
like you), that she didn't know her worth or his truth, that she realized

too late the horrific reality of what she'd wished for in desiring
obsession, and he revisited the dread of his nature like Frankenstein's

monster. What does it mean about pain that it's archetypal,
now that I understand what you meant when you said you had a type?

THE SEARCH FOR MEANING AFTER BEING RAPED

I often think of those *Saw* horror movies—
some hapless dupe kidnapped by a psychopath,

facing gruesome escape puzzles or torture and death.
They have to ask themselves what survival is worth.

Those who lived greeted a gratitude for a world taken for granted,
the dusty pollen of rebirth's bloom after the deep freeze

of a long winter. Sometimes I think of an old news story—
a toddler who fell in a well. Days passed as rescue efforts failed,

as onlookers gawked and gasped. You were born cast-off
into a well, weren't you? No one came to save you, did they?

You grew into a horror to claw your way out. What meaning
do you make of a child, standing on the edge of a void,

a terrifying vacuum of love that threatens to seal off, to swallow
them, unless they find another innocent to push into darkness?

WARNING SIGNS

There were the times you'd show up
right when I got home. Or that time
I told my friend we should get the mail,
and there you stood in a cloud of cigarette smoke
like some dark spirit I'd manifested.

There was that time I was smoking at night.
Slow footsteps crunched dried leaves
behind me. I stood, watched a shadow
scurry around the corner, thinking,
That looked just like the maintenance man.

Who would do that?

No one would ever do that. I googled,
What motivates a stalker?
                It read, *Despair.*

HAUNTINGS

There are details that my mind can only alight momentarily
before the whole flock of thoughts fly off like startled pigeons.
Like the fact that I'd put a conditioner treatment in my hair,

so I was wearing a satin bonnet to bed, or my secret:
that I never stopped sleeping with a teddy bear.
So that's how you found me after drugging me—unconscious

and ugly—gripping a toy like a child, because no one
else would hold me. When I think of the fact
that you had to take my bear out of my clutch to rape me,

my mind turns to cold granite skies before a storm;
thoughts of suicide run through me like a tornado strike.

My breasts hung out of my bra. My bear was on the floor.
My blankets covered me to my chin. How can that be?

After you raped me, you tucked me back in.

RED WEDDING

I told you I'd been raped before;
you seemed empathetic.

You seemed proud
of my strength, remarking
that I turned my pain
into art, my poison
into pollen.

And then
you raped me.

You smirked after
you raped me.

That hatred, that betrayal,
as unexpected, as ruthlessly sharp
as the blades of the Red Wedding.

WATCHING *ANCIENT ALIENS* WITH MY RAPIST

Once, we smoked together. You wanted to watch *Ancient Aliens,*
explaining how Mayans made accurate models of airplanes.

What we had in common: we chain smoked like we had a death wish.
And darker compulsions in our families: rapists, murderers, incest.
I pointed out that these gnarly wounds we bandaged with substances
had been gangrene ever since colonization: my ancestors—enslavers;
yours—Mexican, native to the stolen land. You looked spooked,
maybe realizing I wasn't the enemy you needed to slay,
maybe remembering I was. I'd mistaken you for brother, a balm.

I remember how we coughed at the same time: clutching our chests,
just two humans, welcoming foreign invaders, attempting to expel
toxins, gasping for something pure, for worlds beyond pain,
for the release of gravity's hold. What was alien between us?
What was human? You: *I'm so high.* Me: *I'm no longer on this planet.*

IF I COULD ASK YOU ONE QUESTION

Remember when I was asking you question after question, and you
said you felt like you were being interrogated, and you squirmed
anxiously, and then...*you asked me if I had a knife,* and then...*you asked me
if I had a bucket,* and then...I asked what a knife and bucket had to do
with anything because that's how dumb, no drugged, no dumb, I was,
that I didn't even consider you thought to kill me, just like after the first
rape I didn't even consider that you'd rape me again, or again—you
had the most tortured agony and your eyes were searching me and I
was searching you and I can't forget that look—or you—no
matter what I do, but you didn't do it, even though I told you where it
was, you didn't kill me, and it's not because you have limits or morals
and it's not because you saw me as human or that I didn't deserve it
but my life didn't end the way of the crime shows and I'm falling apart
and wondering *why why didn't you do it why didn't you why didn't you why?*

STI TESTS AFTER DRUGGED ASSAULT

The second round of STI tests came back
negative, so I can finally be sure
you're no longer inside my body
in any way. Why then did I wake today
to a whiff of the subtle steely tinge
of the Texas fall air and suddenly smell

your hair? Why did I want to soothe
it like the breath of a newborn's rage?
Why did I feel disemboweled to remember
how you smelled alive but the residue
you left was infestation, a child's corpse—
maimed, vulnerable, terrified, alone—

how I drag the cross of innocence lost because
you'll never grow strong enough to resurrect.

GYNECOLOGIST

You tell her everything before she touches you *there,*
that it isn't personal, but (breathe) you're going to panic,
and (breathe) you're trying to be mature and explain
that this is just what your brain does, that as soon as she touches you
there, (take the tissue, be a good girl), your heart's going to break,
and you're no longer (breathe) going to be an adult (wipe your nose).
You're going to (breathe) be no older than four years old, (speak
clearly). You're going to wail like a small animal snapped in a metal
trap with teeth. This isn't going to make logical sense, (breathe),
but you're also going to be an orphan. You might call out for *help,*
(you loathe to admit this), you try to explain that this is just what
happens (breathe) when someone touches your deepest hurt
like he did. You leave your body and watch yourself reliving
your death. You don't tell her that. (Exhale: don't look crazy).

WHEN I TOUCH MYSELF AFTER YOU RAPED ME

I watch porn of women with minotaurs—half-men,
half-beasts, all demon—I try not to think of you,
but who else would I think of? Who else needs
me more than you needed me? A predator's
hunger is unmatched. The beast orgasms
volcanic lava; the woman calls him daddy.
Your face rises up like alligator eyes emerging
as I stare into a pool of pond scum. I watch
those reptile eyes of hate as I come,
imagining I'm you, raping me, releasing all my shame
into this vile swamp, imagining it was possible
for you, in that moment, to feel pleasure from me,
for my body to have value, for it to be
the only thing that can take your pain away.

FINDING MY STALKER'S OLD INSTAGRAM

"As a general rule, people, even the wicked, are much more naive and simple-hearted than we suppose. And we, ourselves, are too." -Fyodor Dostoyevsky

For a moment, the glow of photos drained my lungs—
to see your face again was to step on a hive of wasps in my head.
I didn't recognize the man in the photos: you dressed differently,
but you wore that same smirk I only saw you brandish

naked, as you climbed on top of me and showed me all your rage.
In photos, you wore it always: what a fool I was to believe your mask—
designed after my own face—to think we were friends, to listen to your
tales and let your agitation produce a pearl of empathy that I placed

in your flesh, as if your shell was strong enough to protect anything.
You had nine friends; your posts betrayed your loneliness—
blurry selfies and captions, "Was worried." I'd misread your muted
mouth as a signal for *hope:* I should've read it as flare calling out for *help.*

I should've realized that sometimes hunger looks like anger, leers
the same way a gladiator does when an exotic beast enters the ring.

SHAPESHIFTER

I stare at old photos of you, confronting images of my demon
to find a wholly new person, nearly unrecognizable every time,
dressed exactly like the person you stood next to. I realize
you were always wandering this world orphaned, searching
for a parent to copy, appease, avenge. Your identity was the first thing
stolen from you, the first thing you learned to steal.
Then it was boundaries. You invaded me like an infant so attached
to its mother's body that it knows her every odor and crevice.

Next, you learned theft of light, how to plummet
innocence into darkness. I pulled a tarot of a bat for you:
you smirked, *I'm a vampire.* And I'm the witch who knows

what cursed you. You morphed into the shape of my wounds.
We said we both loved horror, a mystery to solve, an evil to unmask.

I have nightmares you're crawling into my womb.

WHAT MY RAPIST TAUGHT ME

Everyone seemed to adore you,
but you said you had no friends.
Who do you confide in? Your mouth
twisted into knots, before bitterly spitting,
You can't trust anyone in this world.

I can hardly believe I made it this far with my illusions,
shrouded only by the flimsy iridescent bubble
that naivety shields. The real lessons
were in the horror stories all along, not the fairy tales.

The living dead walk among us, a parasitic feasting,
a girl alone in the woods, the erection of claws on a full moon,
the penetration of the fang.
                    Don't be afraid: cry out
to the crone in the mirror. Let her reflect the bloody truth.

ISOLATING

Once, you were the sweetest child.
You kneeled whenever they told you.
For prayer. For men.

Now, you stand.
Now, you have nothing
but the clean whistle of your agony,

too high for the human ear.
Your flesh, bitten, to reveal the truth:
the tooth-chipping pit of you,

the quick rot of your softness.
Now, if any lonely body
stumbles upon yours,

the wail of your hunger
will be their daily call to prayer.

WHEN

Some days I ruminate, and a question throbs in my flesh like a thorn:
when did Judas know he'd betray with a kiss? When did the thought
form in your brain, *"I will rape her?"* Was it when we first met, between
that double take when I opened the door? Or did you first indulge
in a fantasy that said, *"I will save her?"* Did you dare to delude a dream
of, *"I will love her?"* Did you know it by the times we laughed together?
Did you know it when you told me your hurts? Or did you deem
me yours to wreck only once you heard me suspect your intentions
weren't kind? When did I become your enemy? Was it the day
you nicknamed me *mama*? Or did you smell me the way a vampire
smells the delicious blood of the fae? Could you tell I was a girl
maimed by her parents just like the boys of my youth could?
Here's the scapegoat. Here's the place we put our shame.
Here's the blood sacrifice to wash away our sins.

GET OVER IT

How many people were raped the nights you were raped?
How many children? How much worse were their rapes
than yours? Is it worse to remember it all?
What's a penis in a vagina? What are lips?
Why do they make you want to die?
Why do you wake in puddles of sweat?
Why do you vomit in the mornings?
Why is your memory stuck on a loop?
Why isn't your body worthy of protection?
Why isn't your story worth being heard?
What makes your pain special?
Why do you love people so much?
Why don't people love you back?
Why don't people love you back?

CHRISTMAS AFTER RAPE

My friend's children are paranoid
that their Elf on the Shelf surveils
their misbehavior. I think about the fact
that I will think about the venom
that paralyzed me forever,
but my stalker's eyes
have slithered away
to choke out new prey.

I used to cry watching
It's a Wonderful Life,
wondering if I'd ever be loved
enough to be rescued from suicide.

Now I know the only person
who'll save me is myself.

HUNTED CARRION

In East Texas, the vultures' hunchback stare, starving
and relentless, pierces like a beak to the gut,
as if they know something I don't. They circle in flight,
stalk from telephone poles, glare in a way that accuses:

Don't you know you're already dead? It's what my stalker smelled—
the decomposition of the girl my parents killed.
When he swooped and fed, I knew the truth of myself:
that I've wandered this earth as an orphaned ghost-child

searching for the parents who killed me, eager to be enfolded
into the black wings of beasts. Daily, I rise
from my grave and stumble obliviously along the same path.
I show my wounds to the living and they recoil, urge

me to walk towards the light. The concrete burns.
I swat off flies. A hungry man waits.

SCAVENGER

How did it taste, that first plunge
of beak into entrails, that squirming

maggot down the throat?
Did it meet your every sick fantasy?

Did it quell your hunger and rage?
You're lucky I make you a vulture

rather than put your name beside your shame.
People would judge you if they knew

your kink for rot and decay.
They'd call you pathetic, a pervert.

If they could see the way you feasted,
they'd recoil to watch you pluck at

my limp body. They'd say, *What kind of beast
can be filled by roadkill? How can it nourish you?*

WHEN PEOPLE WHO ABUSED YOU IN THE PAST FIND OUT WHAT HAPPENED TO YOU

What is it now? Why have you returned, acting
like a devoted mourner to a grave? Is it my survival

you seek to destroy? Or is it my pain you want?
Is it that reek of the carrion that draws you in

just like it attracted him? Who knew my agony
was my greatest seduction? (They knew). Do you remember

all the ways you maimed me, how you cast me off
like my love was nothing but brittle bone,

nothing to feed you? Are you here to pilfer
what's leftover now from the last beast

who picked me apart? Will you finally fly away
for good when you see that this one consumed every last

bit, that all he left for you or anyone else is my skeleton?
And what then? *Will you starve?*

VULNERABILITY

One woman remarked,
He wanted to feel the power
of having your life in his hands.

The shiver that ran down my spine
was so cold it was metallic, unzipping
me inside out, as I felt my body slack
beneath his, how easy
it would've been to kill me.

I remember the way I greeted him
happily, how he'd casually waltz in
when called to fix appliances,
how he'd crouch and pet my cat.

She loves everyone, I said.
She'd crawl into the lap of the devil.

THE WORST SIDE EFFECT

of
being
raped
is
people
will
insist
you
deserved/
wanted/
liked/
misremembered/
fabricated
pain.

VICTIM BLAMING

Some people
blame me
for being drugged
and raped
by my neighbor
who broke into
my home.

That's how I learned
the truth:
how many
rapists
there are,
how broken
our world, our home.

SELF BLAME

Every Saturday night, my best friend and I
texted over the latest episode of *Dateline*.
We joked that it taught the lesson they don't write
in children's books: *Men will try to kill you.*

I got a psychology degree, read books on serial killers—
I never wanted to end up the frozen smile of school photos,
my life a voiceover's lilt of warning and suspense. I didn't want
to be the kind of naive girl to swoon for the charm

of Ted Bundy. The TV shows report how the neighbors
loved them, how generous and attractive people found them,
but they look deranged in their photos, the haunting music
cued every time their face appears. In real life, no music follows

as they approach; their beauty is like a hallucinogen, their warmth
is like the womb, their attack is like the sun vanishing, never returning.

SURVIVOR

In the TV shows, the victims
are described
as beautiful, loving,
full of promise, their deaths
grave injustices—
not deserving any of it.

In real life
you learn
this description
will never be applied to you.

This is only for the *good* girls—
the ones who followed the script.
The ones who did as the audience
craved: *the ones who died.*

DENIAL

I wake early—a new dress, two French braids,
my favorite ring. A thought passes like a cloud
on a breezy day: *I'm glad you happened to me,*
because I'm strong enough to survive you and others aren't.
I teach joyfully, pour all the love I wish I'd been given
into my students. My favorite is despondent.
She stays after, shuts the door—

My stepdad molested me last night.

A flash of light and you bullet my brain, hidden sniper.

She weeps, shivers: *I thought he was my friend.*
I found a peephole: he's been spying on me undressing…

I can't bear to look at her shame—the revolting rot of this wound.

The horror to look upon it and recognize my own face staring back.
The horror to reach to stop her bleeding to discover my limb vanished.

THEN I HAD TO REPORT IT

I realized, again: this is a trap. Authorities will ask what underwear
she wears to bed, if she's sure she didn't want it. They'll assure
this is protection, demand she be raped again before their eyes
before she earns her right to safety. She'll bare her shame
to people who accuse her of lies, a sick need for attention.

You do need attention, dear child—you need mental health care,
a hug from someone loving. You need a break to process
the cognitive dissonance, the Stockholm syndrome, the PTSD.

The word "victim" is a threat to the egos of those deluded by power.
How many in this world envy innocence with such fire that compassion
is consumed? The last thing my student said: "You're the only person
keeping me alive." Then she dropped all her classes.

I can feel the part of my heart infested with hate for rapists—a cold
breeze of rage: *If no one will hear me, I'll slit their throats so they can feel me.*

CORPSE BRIDE

In some places, girls are made to marry their rapists.
This used to strike me as barbaric, until
a man broke into my apartment and raped me.

I imagine our marriage bed the same way
a rash of suicidal thoughts migrate across my flesh
like a flock of crows. What difference would it make?

My bed is my coffin now, a corpse bride.
If another man were to ever reach for me,
my rapist will be there as maggots in my heart.

If I ever sleep next to a man again, my rapist
will be there as my trust clenched into a fist,
wondering if he'll kill me in my sleep.

I've finally learned the secret to make a man happy:
die for his desire, keep breathing, and die again.

STIGMATA

I never predicted my hair would be in the fist
of a man who collected pieces of me as souvenirs,
had a shrine with my underwear, my childhood videos;

never thought I'd live in a sick man's fantasy—
so real that he felt he had to kill it; never
imagined a stalker could be handsome,

could flinch guiltily when I argued
that parents did astonishing work fucking us up;
never envisioned a stranger could kidnap

an inner child so he becomes Father,
Son, and Holy Ghost; never prophesied
my wrists up, post-resurrection, bleeding

my shames, watching strangers flinch
as if before a witch.

THE ROOT OF SUICIDAL THOUGHTS

Nothing will make my rapist
feel remorse
or believe
he shouldn't have done
what he did.

My agony
would make him happy.

Revealing his shames
would make him angry.

Speaking my truth
will make him blame me.

There are many people
who completely
deny humanity.

THE TRICK OF LIFE

They don't teach you
this, but some kids
figure it out
really young.
The rest of us
find out
too late:

The most
dangerous
thing
to be
in this world
is a
loving person.

WHITE NOISE

He's still out there and he wants me dead.
He's still out there and he wants me dead.
He's still out there and he wants me dead.
He's still out there and he wants me dead.
He's still out there and he wants me dead.
He's still out there and he wants me dead.
He's still out there and he wants me dead.
He's still out there and he wants me dead.
He's still out there and he wants me dead.
He's still out there and he wants me dead.
He's still out there and he wants me dead.
He's still out there and he wants me dead.
He's still out there and he wants me dead.
He's still out there and he wants me dead.

DO SOCIOPATHS FEEL REMORSE?

The power went on and off the day I met the man who raped me.
Cold showers and no internet, a chill and isolation to my bones.
By Christmas, it was my heater: an inferno I sat in for days.
He said, *You must have angels watching over you, because this should've exploded.*

Months after, a catfish social media request, a single post:
Remember, you can't consent if you're drugged. He must've been feeling
powerless to need this gloat. I used to crack jokes that made him laugh,
but they were nothing compared to the sneer he wore plundering me.

What Bermuda Triangle inside him swallowed the light I poured
into his pure darkness, the life rafts I flung towards his traumas?
A demon scampers at light, flees towards a shadow to cower in.
An angel never trembles at the sadistic smile of a demon,

never expects it to be anything other than its nature:
an orphaned child, lonely, pitiful, ordinary, godless.

STUDYING THE MENTAL HEALTH OF SERIAL RAPISTS

Did you know they're just like us? Did you know they binge Netflix,
have theories on politics and alien life? Did you know the average
stalker is married, employed, loved? Did you know the majority
of rapists rape inside the victim's home? Did you know they make
home the most dangerous place aside from your body? Did you?

Or was that a surprise, like the way they can ooze sex
from a subtle cock of the hip or that half can't maintain an erection?
Did you realize rape is rooted in humiliation, power, hate?
Did you think it was desire? Did you realize it's self hate? Does that
even make sense? Did you know their illness roots in childhood?
Did you know their brains command horror to survive rage?

Did you know their skin radiates a heat that singes,
that they smell as musty as an infant's foul yawn? Did you know
they sometimes look like your father? Did you know your father?

TRIGGERED MEMORIES: DENIAL

I thought my father was the greatest man alive.
A pilot, a veteran, a hardworking American hero
of the middle class. At three, I clung to his torso
on a motorcycle as he taught me what near-death
and putting your faith in a god felt like. At nine, I gripped
a vomit bucket as he introduced me to flight. I looked
upon the world from a god's eye view. The sins I forgave him:

the belts to my back, the rages, his obsession with staring
out the window at black children, the times he called the police
on them when they were innocently playing,

the time he discovered I was dating a black boy,

how he shrieked and cried, how I didn't recognize
his accusations were actually confessions—*They grow up
to be rapists, treating people only as holes for their dicks.*

WHY GOD?

When I discovered my father
is a rapist
after I'd been stalked
and raped by my neighbor,

I burned his photos.
I cried for days.

It wasn't the first time
I'd been raped—

It was the fourth.

That wasn't counting
the things the lovers did.

The sins of the father.
The sins of the father.
The sins of the father.

CHILDHOOD PHOBIAS

My earliest nightmare was a recurring one:
I'd wake screaming for rescue

from a man with no face.

Before bed, I untucked my sheets, wrapped
them carefully around my body like a mummy.
I believed this would protect me if a snake
crawled into my bed at night.

I'd awaken to something slithering
against my skin, fling myself from bed.
I'd never even seen a snake in person.

But I was convinced: someday a snake
would come for me in my sleep.

Now in my dreams he has a face;
it's his soul that's only a rattle and hiss.

PEOPLE SAY I'M SMART BUT

I actually believed all people were capable of love.
How dumb is that?

I watched specials on serial killers
and I still believed this.
How dumb is that?

I'd been raped before
and I still believed this.
How dumb is that?

I had to believe this
to survive my father.
How dumb is that?

I opened the door and smiled at the man
who'd drug and rape me for weeks.
So dumb I almost died.

PROCESSING TRAUMA WHILE THINKING ABOUT MY CHILDHOOD BOYFRIEND WHO KILLED HIMSELF

We were just two 90s kids in a dingy Midwestern trailer park
where nothing really happened, but everything happened
that would shape me for the rest of my life, and you happened—
you detonated—it happened like an atomic bomb,
and none of us could escape that poison, even when I ran off
and moved to a big city where everything happened,
where I comet-blazed for years, as drunk or high as I could be
to blot out the men who mauled me—that reminded me
of what I wanted to escape—and then everything happened again
and again until I moved to a rural town in the south
where nothing happens—really, nothing happens here—
I've spent a whole year doing nothing, so why am I splitting
clean in half, the hot blade of memory severing me
like a block of butter, like all that happened never stopped happening

TRIGGERED MEMORIES: GRIEF

When I was 15, the most beautiful boy in the world
came to my window, throwing pebbles, asking me to come out.

He'd tell me he saw what I was doing at night, peeping.
After I kissed him, he told me he lost his virginity

breaking into a girl's house, raping her, stealing all her music.
I thought it was a joke. His eyes begged for something.

He said, *I hope I never hurt you,* as if he begged himself.
He said his father was the worst person in the world:

he was named after him. His cousin said he was gay.
He didn't touch me like he was. His best friend accused him

of coming onto him. Then he killed himself. I wanted to crawl
into the casket with his corpse. The last I saw him,

he held me, told me I could be something someday.
He kissed my forehead. Then he took all the music away.

EPIPHANY: MY FATHER'S SINS

Are
Why
He
Tried
To
Kill
Himself

Are
Why
My
First
Love
Killed
Himself

EPIPHANY: MY GUILT

You
don't
have to
keep
blaming
yourself
or your
love
for not
being
enough
for them
to want
to stay

HATE AT FIRST SIGHT

My first love looked at me
dizzy eyed,
kept saying
I reminded him
of his mother.
She abandoned him.

My stalker called me *mama*
every time he said hello.
He said she threw tarot
and did voodoo like me.
She molested him.

I reminded them
of their first love:
a damp, empty well.

UNEXPECTED TRIGGER

While showering, my hand grazes my nipple.
An electric shock zaps between my legs.

A thought: *The last hand to cup my breast*
was my rapist. Another: *He'll be the last*

to cup my breast ever. Next, I'm on my knees
watching vomit and soap suds crawl towards

the drain. I thought that only women
could be gorgons—the enchantment of beauty

corrupted by a nest of snakes, a look of lust
that turns all to stone. But some men

have a touch that transforms the living
into bronze casting, made solid by the hell

of hatred. Their touch, a contagion,
a plague, a doomsday of skin and sin.

THE EMPATH

It's always the rot stench of the wound
that draws me in—the beetle to the Corpse Flower.

You were eager to unfurl your bruised blooms:
you told me about the poverty, the prison, your abusive,

alcoholic father. You winced to mention him. A palpable
stab. I ached to smell more of your festering, to share how it feels

to be birthed of betrayal. I wanted to open myself up
to you like a trench coat, show you the ax to my gut—

my mother. My vanished leg—my father. Now,
I wonder if the stalking, the drugging, the rape

was your wound reveal: *This is the ghost
of my dead inner child. I'm here to show you*

what can happen to children and how bad it can get.
The blood and feces in my sheets said, *This bad.*

ALL THE RESEARCH SAYS

that the surefire way to create a violent, serial rapist is for a mother
to take her baby, swaddle him, wipe him, feed him, & molest him.

For her to raise him in the gaslight of seduction, of getting his needs
met through favors, through being her emotional security blanket,
her handsome knight. All the research says that predatory stalkers

look for women who are overly maternal, innocent like a child.
When caught, they report that victims were "dumb," "asking for it."
They often admit to having a "type," to hating their mothers,
to hating women, to fathers as namesakes who left them for dead.

The research doesn't say anything about how victims process trauma,
how I remember the seductive way you always called me "Mama."

It doesn't say anything about how in my darkest moments of grief,
I ache to take you in my arms, a baby corpse, to ease all your fear
with a lullaby in your ear, *I'm so sorry for what happened to you. Mama's here.*

HAPPY BIRTHDAY, DEAR RAPIST

Sometimes I imagine the day you were born. I was 7,
somewhere in Kalamazoo, Michigan, watching my father

paint model planes. *Tell me about girls who flew, Dad.*

If you try to be a girl who flies, no man will love you.

Somewhere in Mathis, Texas, you took
your first gulp of air and choked, unleashing

your first cry of many cries, as your mother's palm
cupped your backside, the first time of many times.

Nobody knew I'd be a writer. Nobody knew
you'd be a stalker, a rapist who drugs women.

No way anyone could've known: that infant's wail
would be the demonic possession of every pronoun I write.

That pursed pout would be the sleep paralysis apparition,
teeth to tits every morning, hissing, *you'll never fly.*

APOCALYPSE

Most days,
I can't understand
how all of us
can go about our lives
as if there aren't children
in adult bodies
who've been so hurt
they're no longer human.

As if there isn't a loveless void
of rage in them, threatening
to eclipse all light and life.

As if they aren't everywhere.

As if anything could possibly
matter more to our survival.

ANNIVERSARY

Today is the day in which I'll have survived without seeing your face
for the same amount of days in which I knew you: eight months.

I thought today would mean something, a marker in this marathon
of healing. But the truth is I see your face every day and night.

You're a virus, morphing and resisting and attacking with different
strains: abused child; man who wants me dead; baby searching

for a mom; man who craves vengeance; boy who's afraid;
man who smelled like my father; vampire who fed on

my slack neck offered to bloody lips. Now, I drift off
searching for the blank spaces of those drugged moments:

where was I if not in my body? What chill ran through the room
when you had me most vulnerable, when you climbed atop

and could do whatever you wanted? When you took me in hatred,
I understood the concept of being bound until death do you part.

JUDAS KISS

Nothing about the suffering
of the betrayed is new.

You can't convince me that Judas
wasn't a narcissist.

Remember that Narcissus *died*
staring at his own reflection—

of thirst, of starvation.
There was no real love

to nourish him in that mirror.
When Judas faced his truths,

he hung himself.
No amount of gold

can make lovelessness
have worth.

ECHO AND NARCISSUS

The ancient mythology warned
the dangers of loving a man in love
with himself. Echo assisted Zeus' infidelity
and was cursed to never speak her mind again,
doomed to waste away for a man
who wasted away for himself.

Even all the prince charming tales warned
that people hate the naive girls with beauty
and innocence. They're hexed and hunted.

But they also promised those girls
ended up rescued, happy, loved.

The truth is only her bones remain.
She can only repeat the last words
those who can't love her say.

YOU COULD WRITE A BOOK!

Every time I tell someone and they say,
You could write a book,

bile sparks in my belly
like freshly lit coals.

I stand barefooted atop,
accused witch set to flame.

Do you want to know
what he taught me?

Creation is always birthed
from annihilation.

I have to turn his poison
into seed or he'll kill me

and all that I birth. Do you know how hard
it is to spin straw into gold?

ONE OF THESE DAYS, I'D LIKE TO NOT THINK OF YOU

The other day, I held up a garnet and told students the myth
of Persephone, kidnapped by Hades, how she ate a pomegranate
in the underworld: a garnet was the stone pulp she swallowed,
and now she has to be married to the devil for half the year.

She's why we have winter, seasonal deaths, regenerations.

This was my way of confessing that my mind lives always half in hell.
This was my way of introducing you, my husband—the demon
I see when I wake—a gasp I'm still alive—and before I sleep—

a double-check of locks and cameras. I can't tell them your face
is the face I see in the boys with their cowboy swagger, their southern
accents, their effortless charm. So I told the story of Noah:
when the flood came, there was no sun. A garnet was the only light

God provided. How could a rock give light? You have to just believe
light is there, even when you're drowning. That's how faith works.

GHOST HUNTS

The college I teach at is haunted: the tough rodeo boys saunter
to class sleepy-eyed, earnest that poltergeists keep them up at night.

It was a prison for Nazi POWs. Before, a native tribe slaughtered
extinct. Security leads ghost hunts—we show up wide-eyed, high

on adrenaline, gather around an app to ask questions, just like our
ancestors huddled around spirit boards. We see shadows dash

the stage, jump as chairs fall over, laugh as we mistake each other
for ghosts. At home, a crash in my hallway, cats growling.

I suspect even beyond the grave the wounds of the prejudiced fester,
still terrified that they can only uphold their power through violence.

I conjure the image of my rapist and my father. I stand on both spines,
tell the ghosts they found me too late: my fear died to survive

the tripwire of the devil, severed at the ankles so I could never flee.
It was always them who should be afraid of me.

REVENGE

I think
nothing
would
anger
you
more than
knowing
I feel
more
sorry
for you
than
I do
myself.

A BORDERLINE'S LUCID DREAMING

In the dream, Hecate and her dogs greet me at the gates of Hell.
I wear a gown of my own blood, coating my naked body, trailing
a long train behind me. She leads me through dark tunnels to Hades
on his throne of skulls: my groom waits. It's you—so handsome
in your white tux, stained with my blood and lipstick.
I should've known the end of the agony of love would be death.
You flash the same smirk as when you raped me.
Persephone appears, grabs my wrist, and thrusts me into a maze.
Where's my groom? I ask. She opens a trapdoor and I see you:
in bed with another victim. *Don't you understand?* she says.
When you're married to a demon, you're always captive and always alone.
That's what it means to be Queen of the Underworld.
Come, I'll show you how to navigate being eternally lost
in the labyrinth of marriage to the darkest pain.

ONE YEAR LATER: PANIC ATTACK

When my heart sprouts hands
and grips its prison of bones,
knuckles rattling my ribcage,
when I can hear
its desperate pounding
for release, for freedom,

I think it's a miracle
that it hasn't stopped fighting
with every memory
of every thrust of your rage,
that it wasn't stilled
by the sticky venom
of hate you injected
into my womb.

TWO YEAR ANNIVERSARY

I know I'm a ghost because I'm obsessed
with revisiting the place where I died,

because some days the spring air smells exactly
like it did that day, and it fills my lungs

the way the sudden scent of smoke fills
a room when a poltergeist comes to prank.

I comb through every memory—rewind, play—
studying every word for proof of possession.

Each night, I crawl into the bed where I died and pray
I might rest in peace, but it always ends the same way:

I get raped, I get raped, I get raped, I get raped.
Strangers get spooked and tell me I'm dead.

No matter where I turn, I can't find the light.
Hatred is love trapped in the anger stage of grieving.

BECAUSE OF PTSD, SOME NIGHTS

I'm a haunted house. The winter solstice—
the longest night. A freezing storm howls,
ghoulish. Foundations creak, everything
sounds like it's breaking, then sounds
like a child howling. Is it me? Or you?
The power goes on and off.

Some nights I tell myself you drugged me
to protect me from the memory. I tell myself
this to survive the fact that you poisoned me,
that I could've died, that you don't care
about my pain or my poems. That's the point
of storm: devastation. Then, work: regeneration,
to know the divine power and grace
in the balm and miracle of sun's return.

DEATH

I was born and cast into an abyss.
Home was a black hole that hungered
and sealed off all light that entered.
My heart was a leaky balloon, stretched
to its max, lips around a hose.

All my life, I was in love with a man I didn't know.
He hunted me in dreams and his face was a blank canvas.
Then one day he showed up at my door,
and I recognized him as sure as I recognized
the wreckage left of me after love.

When his eyes alighted, when his eyebrow slithered
upwards like a serpent, as he fixed upon his target,
his hunger, I knew the name of my betrothed:

Death.

***

They say Death walks through walls in a grim reaper cloak
with a scythe, but Death knocked on my door
in a backwards baseball hat, a sleeveless t-shirt,
and dirty jeans, holding a new fuse.
Death was the most attractive thing I'd ever seen.
Nothing made me feel more alive
than when Death knocked.

He called me by my real name: Love.

He eclipsed slowly, seductively, like the moon
does the sun. I didn't know He was Death,
but I could feel Him in the pulse between my legs.
I could smell the way the air went stale
when He rushed passed my body, opened
my closets to inspect the rotted guts of my home.

***

The thing about Love is She seeks
to find your deepest wounds to heal you.

The thing about Death is He seeks
to find your deepest wounds to destroy you.

Oh Death, how different I'd thought you'd be.
How much more terrifying.
How much less sad.
I'd romanticized you, irresistible Romeo.

When His skin touched mine,
it was electric shock therapy.

He rendered me unconscious—I didn't see it coming—
He came into my room at night and he gave me
exactly the Death I'd feared and desired since childhood:

in the arms of a vampire.

***

Death can be merciful too,
like a doctor re-breaking a bone to reset it
so it'll heal right. He whispered,

You won't survive this world with this pain…

Like a hunter who found a half-dead doe in the road,
struck by a car—firmly, he snapped my neck.

The real shock is what Love can make Death do:

I repulsed Death.
I made Death weep and rage.
I made Death quiver in fear.

I never realized how powerful I was
until Death showed me what Love did to Him,

until one ordinary morning, I woke with blood
and feces and semen in my sheets.

***

I realized, *my God, I died*—just like that—
and here's the afterlife.

Death came to my bed again and again,
a stoic mourner to a casket.
Sometimes He kissed me.
Mostly He punished me.

After Death comes, He impregnates you with pain.
You rise a ghost, learning to walk in the new world
with a supernatural sight in which you can see the shape
of everyone's secrets and terror.

You approach the living to tell your story.
They startle as if before a monster.
It takes a while to realize you're not alive;
you're perpetually reliving the tragedy that took you out.

***

Eulogy:

Deep down,
the energy
of love
yearns for
death.

Deep down,
the energy
of death
yearns for
love.

Both feel like an erasure
of agony,

an erasure of self.

***

You miss Death, because He's the last thing
you held when you were alive.

Once Death visits, He owns you.
His shadow trails you everywhere.

You gaze down at the open cavity of your chest
and watch maggots squirm as they consume
all the human remains of love that plagued you.

Once Death visits, there's nothing left
to fear anymore. There's no more pain.

Because there's nothing but pain.

Death takes the body, reveals the magician's
vanishing act: it can never touch a soul.

Sawed in two, you somehow walk again.

The resurrection begins.

LETTER TO MY STALKER ON THE TWO YEAR ANNIVERSARY OF MY RAPES

L—

 Healing is like blooming, and these poems were just the first leafy tongues coming out of the dirt where you buried me.

 When you raped me, it was like you surgically opened every repressed wound. I truly felt as if I died.

 The aliveness of my body confused me, going through the motions of living made no sense in a world which had gone so dark. I often questioned if I did die during those nights, if you killed me, and I walk through the afterlife of Hell.

 Then there was the resurrection, a view in which I could see you more clearly.

***

 When you were at my apartment fixing appliances you broke, you said you loved mysteries: you liked to see if you were smart enough to figure it out.

 You've been the greatest mystery of my life.

I've put so much together, but I still have so many questions.

We bonded over loving *Interview with the Vampire*. You loved Lestat: the shameless vampire who didn't question his ruthless nature, reveled in his power to terrorize and bring death, toying with his food, granting his curse of vampirism even to children who'd grow to resent him for turning them monster.

I loved Louis, the sympathetic vampire, in touch with his humanity, questioning what sense to make of his curse before God.

Your dog was named Cersei: the sadistic, jealous, incestuous, selfish queen on *Game of Thrones*.

My cat was named Khaleesi: the benevolent queen dedicated to a revolution of freeing people from their chains and ending rape — the mother of dragons who could walk through fire.

Your favorite TV show was *You*, the story of a romantic stalker.

You told me you didn't sleep much: "a genius only needs six hours."

You knew exactly what you were.

When I pulled a tarot for you in the weeks you raped me and your card was The Bat, you smirked, said, "I'm a vampire."

That's what you were to me: an epiphany that vampires were real.

You're an incredibly smart, self aware sociopath.

You came to me like the stories of Dracula, standing over my bed at night. You fed on me.

But in fiction, vampires are so much more powerful and beautiful. In reality, they're much more tragic and ugly, a bottomless sadness.

I still can't fully make sense of your curse. I can only articulate what your kiss of death did to me, how it turned me into something supernatural too.

***

While you were raping me, I had a vision in which I disassociated.

I saw myself standing over my bed watching you rape me. Next to me was my dead grandmother and ex-boyfriend, dead by suicide at 15. A guardian angel also stood next to me.

We were stoic.

I knew the truth being communicated: this has to happen. There's a bigger purpose.

My grandmother told me, very earnestly, that I was going to survive. I had to find my strength.

You broke me so fully — you broke my body, you broke my heart, you broke my mind, and you broke my whole life.

There isn't one area of my life you didn't infiltrate. I'm feeling the psychological effects of the damage still.

And when a person who looks at you with the kindest eyes unmasks to be a monster, it's difficult not to see everyone as capable of potential predation. My trust is ruined: paranoia and agoraphobia became my bedmates.

Still, I see you as the most important thing that ever happened to me.

You plummeted me to a self reflection full of much more clarity. You helped me discover my Borderline Personality Disorder and understand my family's trauma. You drove me closer to God. Thus, this trauma thrust me into deep healing.

Learning about your mental health gave me many epiphanies, and I solved the mystery of my first love's suicide.

I can see how you were nearly his clone, how you're both an avatar of my father.

What you did set me on a path to deep grieving and facing uncomfortable truths, breaking denials, understanding my own mental health, thus understanding myself better and a lot of the horrors in the world.

I was stunned when I watched *You* to see the victim write her best work after being held captive by her stalker.

But she was murdered and I wasn't, which means I have to figure out, every day, how to survive you.

I felt I had to understand how your brain operated differently from mine, so I turned to books and studied. It cracked my heart open towards the light that led me to escape my anger and find forgiveness and understanding of what trauma I triggered in you, and you in me.

***

Knowing you led me to read a transformative memoir, *Shot in the Heart* by Mikal Gilmore, about growing up in a family with Antisocial Personality Disorder.

I had so many lightning bolt moments looking at my own family tree and life tragedies. As I got to the end, I found myself in fetal position weeping for *you*.

Then that grief also extended to my parents, to my first love, to others who abused or betrayed me.

Last year, I said I didn't forgive you because I didn't need to. I also said I'd kill you if I ever saw you again. But in this year's grief, I found who I needed to forgive: the scared, abused child inside of you.

I can see clearly now the inability for you to control your cPTSD, in which you have to project all your shames to resolve them since you can't grieve. I understand your paranoias, delusions, boredom, and rage at the world. I understand your inability to trust or connect when you can't emotionally experience the feelings of others through empathy. I also understand your escape into fantasy.

When my anger towards you finally began to turn into compassion and forgiveness, it was then I realized...

....if I could forgive someone who society sees as unforgivable, then why couldn't I find some mercy and love for *myself*?

In that way, knowing you taught me these deep spiritual lessons about unconditional love and self love.

The depth of the hatred you flung at me reveals the depths of what I triggered in your broken heart: it shows how much you loved me and how much that terrified you.

You taught me that hatred was a grieving love, a child's broken heart.

You made my heart your enemy. I made your hate my muse.

When you raped me, I understood you to be dead. In writing, I could bring you back to life and give justice to your ghost of an inner child by telling the tragic story of what killed you.

What I kept finding in transmuting my pain into art was wisdom.

I started blogging about my experiences and mental health. My writing became more successful than I'd ever dreamed possible. I amassed over 12,000 followers on one platform and 6,000 on another. My work has millions of views. I also finished a memoir.

You killed me and burned off all this dead wood of trauma, and in doing so, you sent me to reach my full potential.

***

I'm thinking of hunters and honor — how a good hunter will make the kill happen as fast as possible in respect for the spirit of the animal. And if a hunter stumbles upon a wounded animal or one caught in the teeth of a trap, the most noble thing to do is kill it.

A year after the rapes, I dreamed I was a deer, writhing on the side of the road. My guts poured onto the concrete, an entangled slime. I was trying to scream in agony but no sound came out. I just writhed my neck, up and down, unable to heal, unable to walk.

Then your truck pulled up.

You stepped out, looked at me, sighed. Then you took my face in your hands and swiftly snapped my neck.

That felt like what you did in real life too.

It was only after you that I started to pluck all the toxicity out and heal my past, that I developed firmer boundaries and resisted abuses, that I left my job, that I grieved and began to understand my childhood, that I truly began to love myself.

Yet, perhaps I give you too much credit and not enough to myself. There's something unsettling about my meaning making: I see stories all the time of people who die at the hands of sociopaths, of people who were raped who die by suicide, of people drowning in their addictions, of borderlines and narcissists whose lives implode spectacularly.

I watch the harm sociopaths cause and that tar of anger starts to boil in my belly again. I still suffer from BPD, cPTSD, and suicidal ideation. There are times when I have memories of you and I feel certain I won't survive this one. There's a pain from you that feels permanent and crippling.

How many victims do you have? How many won't survive?

And how will *you* survive your suffering?

Don't think I don't wrestle with hate and anger.

I feel a persistent grief that I can't heal you the way that I've healed, and I feel a profound desire to try to help victims who may not have the blessing of the awakening I've had, whose grief is a poison they're drinking, the vampire's venom.

***

Realizing that I have empathy for you and forgiving you has been one of the hardest truths to face after so much anger, cognitive dissonance, and trauma.

For the first year, I spent a lot of time understanding and grieving your childhood and my own. But now, I've been grieving another truth that I'd denied to survive your attacks:

That our friendship mattered to me. It was real.

Our conversations, our jokes, our confided traumas, our shared quirks and interests…those all mattered to me.

When you looked at me warmly and said, "We're friends, right?" That mattered to me.

When you became my worst enemy, the grief that I swallowed was the loss of that friend, that wound that goes deep to my core that says everything I hold dear will abandon or destroy me like my parents did. I know we both have this terror — we just have different trauma responses to it.

For as long as I live, it'll hurt me deeply that I lost your friendship.

I know that narcissists don't give closure or apologize: there's never going to be a time in which you feel guilt or regret over what you did or in which you seek to make amends to me. You stalked me so much that you knew me better than *anyone*, and if my heart didn't mean anything to you, then my words aren't going to either.

I had to forgive someone who wasn't even sorry, but in doing so, I found my strength.

You taught me so many fundamental things about human despair.

Abusers before you left me traumatized, but you broke my brain as if you were resetting a bone. I see the world completely differently now, and my compassion grew rather than shrunk. But I grew stronger and wiser from you as well.

If your goal was to break me, that backfired.

I don't believe that people should be pressured to forgive or find the silver lining in trauma, and I recognize that much of my tenderness towards you is muddied by Stockholm syndrome.

But still, I choose to forgive. I choose love. I choose gratitude.

Thank you, my deepest pain:

For the lessons in self love, unconditional love, and grief.

For triggering me to awaken and heal, to achieve beyond my wildest dreams.

For teaching me how to understand my family.

For teaching me how to forgive the unforgivable, even in the face of the most disorienting hatred, so I could find inner peace and let go of anger.

For showing me how strong I am and my worth.

I pray for you every day.

***

Our relationship wasn't like your favorite show, *You*: we had no romance, and you were much more cunning and sadistic than the main character, though just as charming and handsome.

It didn't end the same way either. Miraculously, it was a love story, not a tragedy.

I never thought I'd have any kind of love story in my life, least of all a love story with myself.

I believe we'll hug someday on the other side of all this, without mental illnesses clouding the fact that we should love one another, that humans were made to love one another.

I'll smile tenderly and say, "We're friends, right?"

You'll hug me and say, "Yeah, we're friends."

And neither of us will be afraid.

BURIAL

To my stalker and rapist:
these words are our offspring,
the gothic fruit that sprouts
from bad seeds.

Thank you for teaching me
to explore the shipwreck—
the jewels to be unearthed
and adorned
from the drowned ghosts
of the sea.

I'm sorry for everything
that happened to you
that turned you into
the pain that happened to me.

Anne Champion

is the author of *She Saints & Holy Profanities* (Quarterly West, 2019), *The Good Girl is Always a Ghost* (Black Lawrence Press, 2018), *Book of Levitations* (Trembling Pillow Press, 2019), *Reluctant Mistress* (Gold Wake Press, 2013), and *The Dark Length Home* (Noctuary Press, 2017). Her work appears in *Verse Daily, diode, Tupelo Quarterly, Prairie Schooner, Crab Orchard Review, Salamander, New South, Redivider, PANK Magazine,* and elsewhere. She was a 2009 Academy of American Poets Prize recipient, a 2016 Best of the Net winner, a Barbara Deming Memorial Grant recipient, and a Pushcart Prize nominee. She received a BA in English Literature and a BS in Behavioral Psychology from Western Michigan University and an MFA in poetry from Emerson College. She's been a professor of English and the humanities for 16 years.

Champion experienced childhood trauma and developed Borderline Personality Disorder. She blogs about mental health, abuse recovery, trauma bonding, and cluster b personality disorders on Medium and Quora.

http://am-champion.com

Help and Crisis Lines

- Rape, Abuse, Incest National Network (**RAINN**): 1-800-656-HOPE (4673)
- Substance Abuse and Mental Health Administration (SAMHSA) Treatment and Referral information helpline: 1-800-662-HELP (4357)
- The Crisis Text Line: Text LISTEN to 741741
- The National Suicide Prevention Lifeline: 1-800-273-TALK (8255)
- The Trevor Project: 1-866-4-U-TREVOR (488-7386)
- Crisis Text for Deaf and Hard of Hearing: Text HEARME to 839863
- National Dating Abuse Helpline: 1-866-331-9474